THE
DAWNING OF GODS
PEACE

THE DAWNING OF GODS PEACE

MINISTER DAVID COUSAR

authorHOUSE®

AuthorHouse™
1663 Liberty Drive
Bloomington, IN 47403
www.authorhouse.com
Phone: 1-800-839-8640

First published by AuthorHouse   12/01/2011

ISBN: 978-1-4670-6282-4 (sc)
ISBN: 978-1-4670-6281-7 (ebk)

Library of Congress Control Number: 2011918384

Printed in the United States of America

CONTENTS

THANKS & AKNOWLEDGEMENTS

First and foremost I would like to thank GOD my eternal judge my LORD and savior for saving me from the penalty of sin. He's truly worthy to be praised. He's the very essence of my being, I can do nothing without him, but through him I'm able to do all things. A special thanks to my mother CARRIE M COUSAR, whom beneath GOD there's no greater love. I thank you for your and patience, no one has provided a greater inspiration than you have. For the many times you told me to try JESUS, you've tried everything else; you were right as usual he does work. Thanks to my godmother sister evangelist Mary Hinton, who believed in me when it was hard for me to believe in myself. I could always depend on you for words of encouragement, you've stood as solid as a rock in praise and worship and often stood in the gap for me. I don't know if I've seen a greater faith than yours, thank you I love you. To my spiritual father and mother apostle Bernard Morris, and co pastor Diane Morris. For your prophetic teachings, your many prayers, and not compromising God's word for any man's convenience. Your teachings taught me to hear and see God for myself, and I truly thank GOD for you. Thank you God Bless Amen. To Sister Burnadette Morris, you've always been such a special friend, truly a woman of virtue and great integrity; I've always respected your obedience and humility when it comes to the word, and ways of GOD. Now I understand why you praise and worship the way you do. You truly Love your God!!!thank you. To my two lovely and beautiful daughters Angelica and Britny cloud, for never giving up on your father, even when I wasn't much of a father, I pray constantly for your strength and understanding, both of you have contributed mightily to helping me become a better father. Thank you for my three wonderful grandchildren. May you always be subdued in the presence of his ever loving, everlasting care and comfort. To my pastor, and my biological and spiritual brother in CHRIST, pastor Timothy Cousar, thank you for allowing GOD to let you be the man he called you to be. You're the only person I ever wanted to pattern my life after, and no one has encouraged and inspired me more than you have. GOD saved you for me, so I could be more like him. Thank you for recognizing the calling God had on my life, and giving me the opportunity to utilize my gifts to bring his name glory. Thank you. And last but certainly not least, to Cynthia Dianne Cousar my wife! Thank you for loving me as only you could. Thank you for being there for our kids when I couldn't be. God created an unbreakable bond between us. No matter how many times we've been separated GOD always brought us back together. You've been in my life since preschool, and I'm looking forward to spending the rest of my life with you, serving our GOD faithfully and gratefully. Thank you. There are so many others I would like to thank, so if I didn't acknowledge you it isn't because I'm not grateful for you. Whoever you are, wherever you are, and whatever your contribution might be. Thank you. GOD bless you all Amen . . .

INTRODUCTION

WELCOME TO the DAWNING OF GOD'S PEACE. I am the author minister David Z Cousar, and I'm truly delighted to present this book to you, it's truly an honor and an a privilege. But I must and do so willingly, give all the glory to my lord and savior JESUS CHRIST . . . It was him that inspired me to write this book, and allow my gifts to be manifested to bring him glory; His joy is my strength. So without further a due I give unto you the dawning of God's Peace a composition of poetic and psalmatic poems and inspirational parables, which will release some powerful revelations unto you pertaining to the gospel of JESUS CHRIST. There's no greater peace than that, which surpasses all understanding! No greater joy than unspeakable joy, and no greater love than unconditional love! When GOD'S peace dawned upon me it opens my eyes to a whole different understanding, and gave me a far greater appreciation for the GOD I serve. Now as I lift up my gifts to GOD, it is my hope that they may refresh your heart increase your understanding, and bless your soul! There is no greater peace, joy, love, or understanding than GOD'S able to offer. The joy of the LORD is my strength, as well as it is yours, and in his right hand are pleasures forevermore. So just as he's pleasured me with this masterpiece to bring glory to his eternal kingdom, I now pleasure you with THE DAWNING OF GOD'S PEACE, as we journey together into the prophetic realm, and receive greater revelations from GOD! Now enjoy THE DAWNING OF GOD'S PEACE! DAVID Z COUSAR, author, poet, extrodinaire, poetry that's breath taking, that'll leave you walking on air!!! PAGE 1 title thank you LORD! Thank you LORD for blessing me with the incredible will to live, in your incredible will, and for teaching me, my blessings are not in how much I receive, but how much I'm willing to give. Thank you LORD for keeping me, when I couldn't keep myself, and also LORD for anointing me with your spirit, which is the abundance of your wealth. Thank you LORD for being there when those obstacles seemed to great, for removing those stumbling blocks from before me LORD without any debate. For being all to me LORD that I've ever needed you to be, I lift my hands and cry holy JEHOVAH in the highest decree, thank you for being LORD over me. Your grace is oh so sufficient 'LORD' your mercy ever so great, I pray that you not depart from me LORD though I'm running a little late!!

TITLE OPPRESSES US NO MORE

WHY MUST we continually fight for equal rights, when we're all made equal in JESUS sight, aren't our four fathers too of the light. Why'd we even have to sit at the back of the bus, the same GOD you claim to serve is the same GOD we in trust. Do you not feel any shame, to oppress us, and have us believe the devil's the blame. Oh what a dangerous game you play, the day will come when you must pay, and I pray that GOD doesn't take his mercy away. Because of your envy strife and greed you kill those of us that are chosen to lead, but GOD still provides everything we need. How can you say this is justified, the many nights our ancestors cried, request unanswered and un-replied. Their only desire to be set free, instead led away and lynched from a tree, in this land we call democracy. Land of the free, home of the brave, where you brought our ancestors to make them your slaves. Do you not feel no shame, oppress us and have us believe the devil's the blame, we're only different on the outside, the inside we're all the same. How much longer will it be before all black men are truly free, to be everything they can truly be? Black men free your minds! Take off the shackles and chains, the shackles off your feet, take the shackles off your brain, we've endured the pain, everything taken from us shall be restored in 'JESUS NAME'.

STARVATION

THIS IS an extended invitation to help end starvation that goes out to every city, country, continent, and nation. As a nation blessed, we must do our best to serve and protect, by showing respect, to those starvation does affect. Starvation comes in many different varieties, and affects us as a society; let us not neglect our priorities. There are nations dying daily from starvation, the most precious of all GODS creations, the degradation of a nation, unwilling to contribute to such a critical situation, are we as much grateful as an ungrateful nation? We set aside for family vacations, but can't spare a dime to help end starvation. Life is the light that shines among every nation, but there is no life without human relations, starvation is in need of world participation!! We have the resources to put men on the moon; universal technology, have they not suffered enough that die from poverty. Are there lives not any more worth that of your own, does anyone really care, GOD has provided us with everything we could possibly need with some left over to share, are we really that selfish we're not willing to share? We have the resources to feed those in need, and there are many still willing to do good deeds, but because of greed many often ever see the proceeds. Poverty doesn't discriminate against any race religion or creed, the next time you have a chance to make a difference whether someone lives or dies just think what if it was your seed. Among the many things we fail to mention, this issue needs our undivided attention. Let's take poverty into apprehension, and put starvation on the list of extinction, share the wealth of divine intervention!!!

I'LL MEET YOU AT THE DOOR

I'LL BE serving the LORD with all humility of mind, leaving all other possessions behind, swallow my pride and follow the signs. I'll continue to serve without any fears; it was his blood, sweat, and tears that allowed me to overcome adversity throughout the years. I magnify and glorify his holy righteous name, he bore my iniquities, that there'd be no more shame, and swore by GOD he'd LOVE us all the same. We know not what befalls, or how long we must reside, only that he that resides in us will never leave our side. Hopefully I might finish my course with joy in the ministry in which I serve, I stand on his promise, and yield to his word, mount up like an eagle and fly like a bird, his voice is as beautiful as any I'd heard. So now as I get closer to heavens shore, I now know what I've been longing for, there's something I desire even more, when GOD opens up his heavens gates I'll meet you at the door!!!! PAGE 5 TITLE LAW OF PERFECTION/ Excuse me man that I'm unreceptive to your laws, but my freedom's in CHRIST who paid it all, the law that's faultless and has no flaws. This law could and would not ever deceive, you can believe whatever, but I forever believe that through this law there isn't anything we can't achieve. This law does not discriminate; it only requires we be patient and wait. This is the law that founded this land, will keep us when none other can. The law that restores all to sanity, that shall judge all humanity, the law that makes and keeps us free, that allows us to be all we can be! So this man is the word I leave with you, the law is GOD and his word is true. Though you justify yourselves in the mist, of your obis and trifling ways, whether or not you obey, this is the only law that shall endure beyond judgment day!!! PAGE 6 TITLE\SILENT PAST\ Who knows how long the soul will last? So that we appear shameless and blameless we pursue a silent past. If we'd humbly reveal our sins today, our past becomes our future, and our sins washed away! Our past is just testimonies, given to you and me, like a light atop a hilltop for the entire world to see. Day in, day out, sun up to sundown, don't let your past keep you bound! Someone's salvation may be in the words that you speak, unless you confess, you'll never know how many you're able to reach, don't be ashamed of your GOD and always continue to seek. If you choose to remain nameless as a name without a face, by eluding your past, you exclude yourself from the race. Though we may run, we cannot hide, for everyone has a past, if we allow ourselves to be redeemed in Christ, our souls will always last!!!

GUIDE US LORD

A HEART WITHOUT direction is a soul without protection. Let your light shine before men, that they may see your good works, that your heavenly father might be glorified, with all humility praise him, and your blessings shall be multiplied, continue to strive for his perfection, let his spirit be your guide, where would you be without the LORD on your side? Lean not to your own understanding nor be overtaken by sin, what profits a man to gain the whole world and lose it in the end? GODS understanding surpasses all understanding, HIS wisdom and knowledge makes a perfect will; a heart without GOD is a troubled heart, one that's yet to be fulfilled, oh taste and see that the LOVE OF GOD is real. There's a time and season for everything beneath the sun, instead of complaining of the things we don't have, let's be thankful for all he's done!!!

THANK GOD FOR THE CHILDREN

THANK GOD for the children, GOD blesses the child that has his own, love them, cherish them, keep them, and make your house their loving home. Lead them, guide them, direct them, pray that they don't go astray, encourage them through faith in CHRIST there will be a brighter day. Hug them, hold them, protect them from the evils that do exist, LORD anoint them in thy holy ways, and dwell there in their midst. And if our children should happen to fall, after doing all we can, teach them that word of CHRIST can lift them up again; they will no longer just be your child, but also your best friend!!!

MOTHER NATURE

IT SEEMS even Mother Nature has a personality of its own. It can be as an angry and rebellious child that has been abandoned and left alone, her rage can be just as strong. Each season seemingly emulates her personalities are more than one; she can unleash the fury of her wrath, or present us with the sun. But who controls Mother Nature and brings about her seasonal change. When she shows us her many strengths how do you think this is arranged? Whether she rains down her much needed rain, or her fury leaves your heart forever stained. It's all a part of a master plan, GOD gave her life as did man. Don't hate Mother Nature for she does that which she must, if you need protection from the many storms give GOD all your trust!!!

WHO'S A MAN?

WHEN DOES a man become a man? From the mother's womb, in the FATHERS hand, from the clutches of the sand, when you're touched by GOD you should understand, HE made us to possess the land. Is it when we've gained great wealth, maintained our health, only GOD can give life you didn't make yourself, but if you don't embrace the life he's given, you can taste the taste of death. We have a choice to make our own selections, only GOD has the answers to all our questions, we only seek GODS face to see his perfection. We should all submit and yield to his plan, a true man is one that has been redeemed in CHRIST to make a righteous stand!!!

PRAISE HIM

MAKE A joyful noise, give thanks to our king, we give him glory honor and praise for the many wonderful things, for those that fear and believe on his name, he shall arise with healing in his wings. Worship him with thanksgiving, lift him up in song, earth is just a temporary dwelling place, he's made heaven to be our home, forever in his presence to worship before his throne. Love him in your heart; honor him in your soul, in the coming of HIS glory, HIS beauty we shall behold. None shall escape judgment as his separation begin, those that receive eternal life will be forever free of sin, those that refuse to answer HIS call shall meet a dreadful end, but do let me remind you, the devil has no friends!!!

PEACEFUL RESSOLVE

WHEN DOES war become necessary does anyone win in the end? One man taking the life of another is just one of many definitions of sin. What's all the fighting for? Why can't we all just get along? If war is the only answer then we're doing something wrong. Wars among brother's, neighbors, and nations increasing budget deficits, economic inflation, creating weapons of mass devastation. Families crying as their children are dying, even those who fight for peace, sadden by the many that's fallen, as the body counts continue to increase, regardless of any indifference we may have the only resolve is peace, GOD made us all to love one another so let the fighting cease

NO MORE WAR

J UST WHAT exactly do we expect to gain, if we don't respect GOD, and expect a change, killing innocent people, and using his name. Our wars are vein, only causing many people so much pain. Pakistan-Afghanistan, which nations of war will continue to stand, if war's the only menu, that's pleasing to man, violence begets violence throughout this land, only GOD knows how this world will end. Joy and peace of the promise, for those whom have chosen CHRIST, those that don't believe, have chosen to roll the dice, their souls condemned and separated from life. Time will soon reveal all universal mysteries, from far beyond the clouds, to the uttermost depth of seas, war is the world's most deadly disease, for this reason many are bred to breed, we should LOVE one another not kill our seeds. How many of us will continue to stand, as we explore our new life in our new land. All power in JESUS hand, GODS perfect will and perfect plan! As we ascend into the heavens, beneath the greatness of his throne, that day surely shall be a day of peace, and the wars will all be gone!!!

GODS PEACE

I N ORDER to bring about peace among nations, GODS peace must be accepted worldwide, ungodly acts are a GOD known fact, your sins you cannot hide. GOD'S word is uncompromised, all knowing, all wise, his peace is something we can't disguise. His voice can speak without making a sound, quake the earth, shake the ground, lift you up or take you down, everything that's lost and needs to be found, His word's not bound, HE raised up our king in glory, and gave HIM HIS crown, GODS peace is sacred ground! Over and over again and again, his peace is real we can't pretend, every man desires peace within, peace for his family and among his friends. He's calling us to come higher, the fire within, the standards of GOD are higher than men, it's HIS desire that we'd all make it in, one nation under GOD forever free of sin!!!

SEEKING UNDERSTANDING

GODS UNDERSTANDING is greater than any could ever concede, seek HIS understanding and fulfill your needs, instill truth in your seed, that their success will be greater, when they do succeed, the understanding of GOD no one could ever exceed! Understanding is something we should always seek, but we should understand GOD before we open our mouths to speak, He's our shepherd, we should follow as sheep, GOD IS GOD, His word is deep, there is no other GOD that could ever compete, in all things it's sown to reap, earth is HIS footstool we're beneath HIS feet. We search the universe for signs of life, while suffering GODS heart much envy and strife, I hunger and thirst for CHRIST, GOD requires obedience over sacrifice. What have I given up that I can't get back, if HE'S given me understanding that I shouldn't lack. Find your reason and purpose, your place in his will, oh taste and see that the LORD is real, it's by HIS understanding, we all are sealed!!!

OBEDIENCE

GIVE IN to the FATHER, accept HIS holy ways, a child that's disobedient will only live to see half his days. None is perfect but the FATHER, it's HE that makes us strong, He's blessed HIS throne, and the child that has his own, He'll never forsake us or leave us alone. HE perfects us in the spirit, with repentance in our hearts, not to be condemned as children of the dark, GOD always finishes that which HE starts, that all that are chosen will reach their mark! Whatever that child decides to do once he gives his heart to GOD, He'll see them through, and bless them in everything they do, stay humble, be true, and let HIM minister to the child in you! He's reserved a place and the rights to every man's soul, hold true to the faith, be faithful in HIS fold, as a child that's bold, our obedience in CHRIST is what makes us whole!!!

SIN KILLS

S IN IS not friendly, sin is not kind, it corrupts the heart and distorts the mind, sin is darkness that cannot shine, if you're still in darkness you're still confined, many there be that cross that line. Every day is a new day, one we've never seen before, today may the day that it comes knocking at your door, it's not a thing our hearts should store, JESUS said repent, go and sin no more. Sin is seductive, it's never nice, before you let it in you better think twice, he without sin, need not a sacrifice, you were bought and paid with a price, for every man's sin JESUS laid down his life. It pits son against fathers, daughters against mothers, no one sin is greater than the other, none greater than GOD who delivers us from all our troubles, it steals the anointing, deprives the man, from going forth to possess the land, chosen of GOD unwilling to stand. Sin is unfruitful it only pretends, how can sin being evil be anyone's friend, rebuke the devil don't dine in his den, only a fool would choose to live and die in sin!!!

LAST TO FIRST

AMAZING UNIVERSE complex and diverse, and shall remain that way until GOD removes the curse, in heaven and earth, the first shall be last, and the last shall be first, GOD'S there for his people, whether better or worse! Though we much war among races, gender, and nations, racism is as much part of life as economic inflation, demonic demonstrations, the enemy uses the world system to elect his administration, to try and rob GODS children of their eternal vacation, the first shall be those of righteous indignation. The last shall be those that do evil deeds, bearing unfruitful and evil seeds, it's not about race color or creed, love sees no color, it only sees a need, to fulfill GODS will by doing HIS deeds. Evil does not discriminate it only knows to hate, without repentance no man's soul makes it through the gates. Those that seek and thirst for righteousness their souls shall be edified, forever uplifted and their seeds multiplied, those that haven't been purged and cleansed access denied, those that trust and believe, with HIM their souls shall abide. Endure the worse reverse the curse, give yourself to GOD and receive HIS purse, though you may have been last, GOD has made you first!!!

LOVE

Love is the reason Jesus was born, and the reason he gave his life, Lord God, Jesus the Christ, there's never been a greater sacrifice, no man shall see his kingdom, with his heart filled with envy and strife. Love is sacred beautiful, and kind, love is not drunken and easy to find. GOD is love, and love is mine. Love endures, until the end of time. Where time ends, eternity begins, GODS love has no end. Love is joy, love is peace, God's love will never cease, plant your harvest in love, he'll give an increase. Love is eternal, love is deep, if it's love you've sown, It's love you'll reap, love you'll keep, his love you'll find, if it's love you'll seek. Love is good, it's never bad the love of GOD won't leave you sad. It does not cheat, it doesn't steal, it isn't void it only fulfills. Love conquers, love endures, a heart that loves is a heart that's pure! Love is bold. Love is strong, it will never forsake or leave you alone, Jesus the Christ our rare and precious stone, endured the cross, inherited the throne, prepared a place he calls our home! Love sometimes scorn, but it never hates, it only seeks to mate, if you've found GODS love, then love is great. Love in every corner of every border, even beyond the sky. Love forgives without asking the question why? And it's only reply, I have more love than any supply, love is everlasting it will never die. The promises of GOD in which we can all rely! Love is the beginning, love is the end, Love Love's it's enemy as well as friends, the only thing it hates is sin, those that have it will always win. Love is the gift of life given to men, eternal life for those who are born again. Love is a many wonderful and splendid things, Jesus Christ LORD of LORDS KING of KINGS. Love is GOD, GOD is love, and love is putting nothing before the father above!

GOD'S WISDOM

GOD WILL destroy the wisdom of the wise, who from the beginning has uttered lies. They twist the scripture, but to their own destruction, they have their own laws, and their own instructions. Why can't we see as he see, if it was liken unto him, he imagined us to be? Even the foolishness of GOD is wiser than man, how wise are we to continue in sin, with the enemy plucking at our soul, like feathers from a hen. If we're not soul out to God, we're sold out to sin! Man's wisdom is only confounded in the Excellency of his speech, if his wisdom is worldly, he's not worthy to teach, his trust is breech, he lust to touch those things that keeps him weak, the gospel was chosen for the chosen to preach, and there are no limits to how far GOD'S gospel can reach. In the power of his might of his mighty hand, HE created this land, and breathed the breath of life into man. Thank GOD for the gift of the Promised Land, and upon this promise, we should continue to stand. God's wisdom surpasses that of every man.

WALK BY FAITH

THOSE THAT are in Christ, walk by faith, not by sight, in the power of his might, even in darkness can still see the light. For as much as the sun is to the day, and the moon to the night, pleasing GOD is my only delight. He's shown me things I never thought I would see, taken me places I never expected to be. Where the spirit of the LORD is there is liberty, the devil has been defeated, we've been given the victory. Oh ye of little faith give thanks unto thee! Walk by faith not by sight. "The truth will make you free." He whom the son sets free is free indeed; GOD freely gives to his every need. It only takes faith the size of a mustard seed, and in all things we endure, and do succeed.

GLORY TO GOD MY ETERNAL FRIEND

W E MUST love one another, as GOD loves us, for ungodly things we should not lust, we can trust him, but can he trust us? Those that walk after the spirit, are the ones he trust. Spiritual things are spiritually discerned, pleasing GOD should be our primary concern, that we're not cast into the lakes of fire, where our souls will burn. Why does man think he knows what best, dwell in sin, but won't confess. No wonder this world's in such a mess. To reign with GOD we must past his test. Give it all to him and our souls can rest. God is loving caring and able, we drink from his cup, and sup from his tables. His spirit makes and keeps us stable. He's the light of the mind body and soul. His spirit is humble, yet so bold, teaches all things, in which we accomplish our goals. Blessed is the man whom he will not impute sin. The heart is evil but GODS word thoroughly cleanse, take the root, and pull it from the end. God the father, Christ Jesus, thy savior and friend, in the coming of his glory eternal life will begin. Everyday shall be as Sunday give glory to our king. The Father, the Son, and Holy Ghost, "God" my eternal friend.

WITHOUT LIMITATIONS

IN THE midst of our own destruction, and devastation, the power of GOD is without limitations. Wherever there's sickness, and suffering, the enemy strides, so shall GOD'S grace and mercy abide. God is a true and loving GOD, he'll never leave your side. Where there's affliction and addiction, those lost to be found, his word's not bound, his doctrine is sound, the LORD will never let you down, he's the living water, no man should drown. Through our many trials and tribulations we all fall short of sin, whether of sin unto death or obedience unto righteous, it's his judgment in the end, on his judgment we can all depend, so utilize wisely the time you spend. It doesn't matter who you are, or what you've done GODS peace will comfort you, he's greater than all of our tribulations combined his spirit will guide us through. Let the old man be cast away. The new man come shining through. Even your most unimaginable dreams, GOD will make them all come true.

A MOTHERS LOVE

A MOTHER'S LOVE is very unique. Like a mountain that has no peek, deeper than fountains of the deep. The best for her child is what she seeks. Her faith is strong when her child is weak, the blessings of GOD, over her child she speaks. Lord protect my child, that he don't die in the streets. Beneath GOD'S love, there's none above, when push comes to shove, she loves her child because she knows it what it does. I must give honor where honor is due, I give glory to GOD, and honor to you, I know you love me. I love you too. Thank you mom for all you've done. Though you raised me in the loving care of GOD, I often failed you as a son. Thank GOD for my mother he only blessed me with one, you've helped me endure every race I've run. I didn't win every race, but it sure was fun. Because I'm always reminded of your love for your son.

GOD'S VISION

BEFORE THERE were plagues, famines, and floods in the land, man was just a vision of the sand, made in the image and likeness thereof our father GOD whom is "love". Fed and bred by his strong hand that we'd prosper through that which HE command. But somehow along the way, we became a people led astray. Even though his mercy and his grace, saved his people as a race, and made their hearts his dwelling place. Wretched minds hardened hearts, and tortured souls, they to shall come into the fold. "You see" in order for his will to be done we all have to become as one. "United we stand". Divided we fall. Isn't it ironic "GOD conquers all"? So I say unto you LORD, in the year of your favor, I acknowledge you as my LORD, and my SAVIOR.

UTTERANCE OF ANGELS

As I sat alone consume in fear, there came an utterance of angels to my ear, with a message from GOD I needed to hear, as my eyes immediately begun to tear. As they spoke, I could hear so vividly, the voice of Jesus saying you've been set free, I couldn't understand why he'd come to me. He said these things are not as they appear to be. Fear not my child those things at hand, but only I that keeps and governs this land, have you any doubt that you can? Though I've given you the strength to endure until the end, shed my blood for remission of sin, now I'm fishing for men, you shall not be bound again. From this perspective, I change your view, and little do I ask of you, acknowledge me to be real and true, and do those things I ask of you. So fear not, come unto me, and receive life throughout eternity.

FREE AT LAST

I'VE SEEN the lightening flash, heard the thunder roar. As the waves of the ocean gently caress the shore. Many times I'd often wonder when my sins would be no more. God knows I hadn't any more room to store. Though I know I've been forgiven, there's a storm that lies ahead. The only way I will prevail is to stand fast in Jesus stead. Yes greater are the blessing, of he that resides in me. Because through those storms came liberty and my true identity, a man that was once broken is now made whole and free.

BLESSED ASSURANCE

GOD is GOD, and GOD alone. And none is worthy of his throne, as he watches over us form heaven above, truly there could never be a greater love. Through our trials and tribulations and much endurance GOD offers us his blessed assurance. His word is our restitution we shall no longer be enslaved, Jesus went to hell and took the keys of death, when he arose from his grave, oh death where is your sting I shall not be afraid. Did Jesus not say in his word stand back and behave. He's our soul provider, our shelter from the rain, his riches, and glory, not fortune and fame. He's my portion, my everything, my blessed assurance, my works aren't in vein, all power in Jesus name. He's brought us from a foreign land back into his fold, not because we do deserve so what pleasure do we owe, when he calls we must answer the roll. He reserves the rights to every man's soul. We'll be dining soon in the upper rooms of Jesus holy estates. No more rats, roaches, or snakes, his divine countenance shall be upon us, as we break bread from his plate. Keep your eye on the prize and claim your stake. Everything we gain is gained through faith. Yes above the clouds there is a savior that watches over you and me. God's blessed assurance shall forever be, and though we may be among the many that's called, it's only for the chosen few to see.

DEMOCRACY

ONLY INDIVIDUALITY of spirituality can reform a nation so why don't we give our politicians. A permanent vacation there laws are just as satanic as Satan. For who and what does their democracy stand, and what gives them the right to divide this land. Chosen by whom and how they can lead when their only concerns are their own selfish needs, for wealth and power they're willing to do the devils deeds. As they deceive and manipulate. Their gender is self, while putting the needs of the people on an idle shelf. Their laws are wicked judgments profound but not enough to keep me bound. The will of GOD is much to sound their gods are cursed, this is sacred ground. It's not their constitution that has made me free; but GOD who has imagined me to be. So when you're headed to the pulls after hearing their debates remember to elect GOD before it's to late. Then shall democracy emancipate.

GREATER IS HE"

GREATER IS he that's the beginning and the end. Greater is he that calls us brethren and friend, shed his blood for the remission of sin. Greater is he that now dwells within. Greater is he that never slumbers nor sleep, greater is the shepherd that guides his sheep, the Lamb of God that humbled himself before GODS feet. Greater is he through divine intervention allows us to give him honorable mention. Greater is he that has renewed our minds that idolatry, and ignorance shall not keep us blind for every mountain he doesn't remove he gives us the strength to climb. Greater is he that's greater than time, whose light will never cease to shine. Greater is he that gave Job the faith to withstand, the wrath brought upon him and his land. Greater is he that rules with a mighty hand. Greater are the vessels that are true and just, that obey GODS word and do as they must. Greater is he that comes from the dust that walks in favor, and has earned GODS trust! Greater is he that imagined us to be, greater is the vision of His prophecy. Mighty are his works, excellent is his name. none greater than he that'll always reign! It's great to know, he'll always be the same!

ARRESTED SOULS

THOUGH MY soul has been greatly battle tested my wounds have healed, my soul arrested, can't give up now, have too much vested. Now I fight for a greater cause to spread GOD'S word; and keep his laws, rebuke the enemy, and tear down his walls,

God knows man won't past every test, but respects the man that gives his best, that loves his GOD, and offers nothing less!

I rejoice in the LORD, who has made me whole,

A prisoner of Christ, an arrested soul!

INSIDE THESE WALLS

I NSIDE THESE walls, there's a voice that must be heard, a witness of the manifestation of GODS mighty word!

Though these walls have been constantly stained, behind these walls, I shall humbly remain. To know GOD is to love him, he wouldn't have you suffer in vein.

Inside these walls are the hearts of men, of whom have fallen again and again.

These walls were conceived, and structured in sin, these walls are the testimonies of many men.

From that innocent child, that doesn't remember his youth, these walls have been restructured, to uphold the truth!

These walls are sustained in Jesus name, behind these walls things will never be the same.

Behind these walls, should I happen to fall it'll only be after I've given my all. Behind these walls are the chosen of GOD, by the powers invested in thee, I'm claiming victory, free at last, free at last, thank GOD almighty I'm free.

COLOR OF BEAUTY

Color of money, color of friends, color of everything, that ever has been, is based on the complexity of skin, darkness is the color of sin, regardless of what skin we're in, there's no greater beauty, than that within, character is the only content, that propels men to GOD and GOD to men!

ME-OTHIC

THE WAYS of the world are so me-othic, vein and gothic, their favorite word is me, they never change the topic, they wear their hearts on their sleeve, and breathe from, their pockets, everything you ever needed in the world, GOD got it, he gave us his word to work as an antibiotic. What he has for you nobody can stop it!

CURSED TO BE DAMNED

WHEN YOUR troubles are double, your heart in a jam, with the cares of the world, cursed to be damned, by the unction of his spirit, his voiced rained down, I rejoiced in the sound, though you were lost, now you are found, because the word of GOD can never be bound, it'll pick you up, and turn you around, you are who you are, because I am, that I am! If all these things thou have conceived, be it unto you, as thou have believed, I am the GOD that fulfills all your needs!

EARTH HAS NO SORROW

PAIN, HURT, AND SORROW, IS A MUCH GAURENTEED, AS GODS PROMISE TO FULFILL OUR EVERY NEED, BUT EARTH HAS NO SORROW, THAT HEAVEN CAN'T HEAL, A PERFECT PLAN, FOR A PERFECT WILL, GOD IS LOVE, LOVE IS REAL, IN HIM, EVERY MAN'S DESTINY, AND FATE IS SEALED! EVERYTHING CREATED BY HIM MUST YIELD! REGARDLESS OF WHO YOU ARE, OR HOW YOU MAY FEEL EARTH HAS NO SORROW THAT HEAVEN CAN'T HEAL!!!!

True Meaning of Love

Sarah bared a child when her womb was beyond bearing,
The burden of Moses speech was passed on to Aaron

Job endured the wrath without ever swearing,

The miracle child the virgin Mary was carrying would put nothing on us that's to overbearing,

Taught us the true meaning of love, sharing, and caring.

Love in a bag

When we dispose of the garbage, and take out the trash, Wouldn't it be so nice, if we could store love in the bag,

Shape our future's from love rather than basing it on the past,

Knowing that those we love, and love us, would always last, pain and sadness could make us happy and glad,

When we think of liberty and dawn our flag,

One man rejoices in his riches, the other rejoice in rags, Thanking God he can't miss what he never had.

Without within, 'truth Christ', sin and men

If I had to tell the story, where would I begin?
Since it comes from inside let's begin within
First there was the word which was God
The truth begins
The way and the life
The root of the plan
He separated the firmament
Created the land
Heaven and earth,
Soil and sand,
From the soil he created him man,
From the nostrils.
Breathed he breath into man,
Began his rule with a,
Great and mighty hand,
Made a promise he'd make a place,
Where life never has to end,
Man failed to comply,
What applied to men,
In comes Satin,
And thus does sin,
Separated from God
Man became without within,
I've been without cars, without money and friends,
I've been without within
Without truth and knowledge,
But never without sin,
Even if the truth offend,
Lord I promise I'll never leave home without it again.

In the midst of it all

Even in hindsight,
Retrospect to it all,
God respects us when we stand,
Though he expects us to fall,
Not a blessing to one,
But a blessing to all,
Protects us,
When we're down and out,
Backs against the wall,
Against the enemy,
None to large or small,
From the valley's lows,
No mountains to tall,
No purpose, no reason
No reason beyond call,
When trouble arises,
And sin befalls,
Above purpose, and reason
Beyond the call,
He's the reason for the seasons
And in the midst of it all!!!

Misled

Beneath the stars,
The skies,
Big City lights,
Shots ring out in the middle of the night,
A mother cries out,
As her son loses his life
Forced to accept,
But not question
Nor contest God's will
Though she never thought
She'd see the day,
He'd die,
And she'd live.
Everything she'd imagined, and dreamed he'd be,
Why'd it have to be him,
Why couldn't it be me,
It was as a dream,
As if she'd been awaken from bed,
Screaming and shaking,
Was it all in her head,
Or had it come to past the one thing she'd always dread,
He'd been misled,
Her child was gone,
Her son was dead,
Only left with memories,
Forced to face the fact,
Her son was gone, and never coming back,
She loved her son, more than you can count the ways,
Now all she could count was the nights and days,
It was the last time she'd hold him, or see his face.

I Am Is Me

I am that I am,
The greatest to be,
IS, ever was, or ever will be,
From the heavens above,
Every mountain, every tree,
The depths of your soul,
To the depths of the sea,
It's the debt of my blood,
That has set you free,
I was destined for you,
As you're destined for me,
From beginning to end,
A to Z,
A billion times, a billion,
Times a billion times three,
If you're looking for a blessing,
Your greatest blessing is me,
I am that I am
I am is me!

For the sake of the soul

Though the storms shall be many
We must weather the storms,
Let your spirit be renewed,
Your mind transformed,
Be of good courage,
Keep the faith,
Never give up hope,
It's never too late,
He'll run your cup over,
Fill your plate,
We all fall short,
All make mistakes,
Always be prayerful,
Be patient and wait, love overcomes hate
There's nothing worth more when your soul is at stake.

Real

In your will,
I have the courage of a lion,
A heart of steel,
Without you,
I don't have the will to live,
Peace be still
Relegated to your will,
Dedicated and committed,
I know that you're real,
Appointed and anointed to do his will.

True friend

A true friend
Won't break or bend,

Watch your back
Through thick and thin,

If necessary
Take blows to the chin,

Rescue you
From a lion's den,

He's there even when
You don't have money to spend,

Neither will he judge you
For your sins,

Be there for you
Till the very end,

When it's over
He'll make amends,

And still he'll do it
All over again.

Divinely ordained

I looked upon his wisdom
In hope of change,
Looked to the heavens,
It began to rain,
He opened up the windows,
Consoled my pain,
Embraced me with his love,
Placed me beneath his wings,
It was evidently plain,
I'd been heavenly sent,
And divinely ordained.

Live for today

All of my yesterday's
Have gone away to stay,
Washed out into the sea of forgetfulness,
My future is today,
Upon my knees I'll continue to pray,
God lead me, guide me, show me the way,
Tomorrow isn't promised
I can only live for today.

Never leave me alone

My Lord, My God
My chief cornerstone
Here I am again before your throne,
I thank you Lord for the love you've shown,
You gave me hope when all hope was gone,
You're the greatest love I've ever known,
My spirit is drawn
Finally I have something I can call my own,
Many are my sins,
And I'm often wrong,
But promise me LORD,
You'll never leave me alone
Reserve a place in my heart
And your heavenly home.

Scorned

From the day I was born,
My spirit was torn,
Not really sure if I was coming or going,
Trying to hold on to survive the storm,
I was told the devil was red and had two horns,
God's the reason and purpose the earth was formed,
Man's loins is where good and evil joins,
Give no thought to what's to be worn,
If you're just not sure you should flip a coin,
If someone dies we shouldn't cry,
It's not the reason we should mourn,
God only knows what's out of the norm,
Fruit that doesn't multiply dies among thorns,
To raise a child the Father sometimes scorns.

Eternal Divide

To every story there's at least two sides,
This is the story of the eternal divides,
There once was a young man who was seeking a ride,
He was tired so he never looked to see who was on the other side,
Once he recognized he tried to run and he tried to hide,
But the voice thunderously cried,
I am the voice of the eternal divide,
I've come to carry you to the other side,
But first your heart must be tried,
The young man opened his heart wide,
And humbled himself from pride,
And he replied,
I'm tired of being denied
I thank you Lord,
And I will confide,
That my blessings may continue to be multiplied,
Forgive me for the many times I've lied,
For delivering me from those demons of suicide,
For protecting me from the many times I should have died,
I've tried everything on the other side

And I know this ride is uncompromised,
But it may be my last chance to reach the other side,
Hopefully my access won't be denied,
Because I know there's something better waiting for me on the other side,
Though the young man had once tried to hide,
It was on this wise,
That he did decide,
To humbly and graciously,
Accept the ride, to forever reside on the other side of the eternal divide.

Perfect

When God has delivered every soul,
That desires to be healed that has sown and reaped,
The harvest of their fields,
I'll be loving life,
Life will be loving me still,
I've been blessed with life twice,
And I know God's love is real,
We must all do our part
To fulfill his perfect will,
Embrace life,
Extend that love to all,
Reserve a place in your heart for life
And surrender when it calls,
Stand tall on the foundation of life,
And it will rebuild you when you fall,
There's only one larger than life,
And he's given life to us all.

Life

When I look back down yonder road,

I see visions of yesterday things seemed as they would never change,

But it was only because I made it that way creating illusions for tomorrow, never concerned
about today.

I can never travel those roads again. The price is too great to pay,

Life is too short and precious, we don't have time to play.

Live long and prosper be fruitful and multiply, Don't let life pass you by. Every man has one price
to pay, and we're all born to die.

If God said it why ask why?

It'll soon be revealed by and by.

Amazing

Amazing universe
As are thy features,
Most amazing is the love,
God has for his creatures,
Continues to teach us,
Though it's sometimes hard for GOD to reach us
Even as Christians, we don't always listen
Is it really worth risking the blessings we're missing,
No matter who you are, or what you've done
God loves his daughters and his sons,
Be thankful for him and all he's done,
His love is deep as the oceans are wide,
Greater than the tides,
Confide in him if you must confide,
Despite your many sins,
He's still on your side.

God's face

Love peace and joy
Mercy and grace,
Above all things
I want to see his face,
We're all different people,
But only one race,
One Lord one God
We should all embrace,
Once you've tasted victory
You know how it tastes,
It's never too late,
Life is too precious
Don't let it go to waste,
God is great but you got to have faith.

Draw nigh unto us

Draw nigh unto us
Keep us aboard,
Draw nigh unto us
We need you Lord,
My rod my shield,
My staff my sword,
One mind, one body, one accord
Make us whole
Fill our voids,
A righteous man shall receive,
A righteous man's reward
With all that I am
I shall serve you Lord.

Still I'm blessed

Sit it off your shoulders,
Get it off your chest,
Count it all joy
Still I'm blessed,
The journey the quest,
Trials and tribulations the eternal test,
The earnings are greater
For those who invest,
As long as there's more
You don't settle for less,
We must all be cleansed
Purged of our mess,
Sowing seeds of discord
Reaping stress, every knee must bow
Every tongue confess,
Give it to God he deserves your best,
You're a special guest
Continue to strive,
Continue to press,
The things I need most I already posses
Love, joy, peace, and happiness
The devil is a lie
Still you're blessed.

Nature isn't technology

Nature isn't technology
No there not the same, one's nocturnal, the others not plain.
I hear the chirping of the birds, the stacks from trains,
I see the soaring of birds, pollution from planes,
The nature of technology is often strange,
Nature offers no explanation, and can't be explained
Where there's smoke there's fire, where there's fire there's flames,
Above the mountains beneath the plains,
Technology's limited
Nature unrestrained
They've both given us joy, as well as pain, but this is about as well as I can begin to explain,
Technology is a thesis, we believe with our brain,
Jesus is the reason all things must change.
Give me the chirping of the birds,
The joy, the pain, rays of sunshine, drops of rain,
The seeds of my crops weren't sown in vein,
My seeds were sown in Jesus name.

Deliverance in Jesus name

From the ghetto and country
Slums of crack cocaine,
I claim deliverance in Jesus name,
I suppose I could walk around with my head
Down feeling shame,
I could accept responsibility
Or place the blame,
Physical, mental, spiritual, stains
I accept responsibility for causing God pain
Right here's the only place
I can place the blame,
Still I count it all joy,
I know it sounds insane,
In order to make difference,
We must first make a change,
I claim deliverance in Jesus name,
Life's too precious, no more living in vein,
Those that suffer with Christ shall also reign.

Uncompromised

From the ruins and ashes,
Of compromise,
Beneath the skin
Where evil lies,
Thank God
He heard my cries,
Opened my eyes,
Only he can make
The foolish wise
From the ruins and ashes I continue to rise
The spirit of God
Is un-compromised.

For the love of this family

We've all fallen short,
Thus thy I have sinned,
For the love of this family, let's make amends,
God bless this reunion before it begins
We come not before you, in judgment of men,
But to give honor, and thanks for family and friends.
Bring us together today as one,
Bless our mothers, fathers, daughters, and sons,
Renew our strengths, our vows, our love, our bonds,
Make it a day of rejoicing, one filled with fun,
For the love of this family,
Let God's will be done.

Atoned

I lay down my heavy burdens,
Put them in your care,
They're much too heavy, for my shoulders to bare,
Sometimes the roads' got rough, beyond compare, but when I called your name you were already there.
I've chosen some wrong paths, but this I pray, my sins are forgiven then passed away!
It's been a long journey,
I took the long road home,
I'd often get weak, then you made me strong,
Keep me covered in your blood beneath your throne,
It's been written in the sand, etched in stone,
Atoned through the blood, not flesh and bone,
If I've ever been right, then this can't be wrong,
You're not just the best, but the greatest love to ever be known.

Masterpiece final destination

Master please give me peace,
That, surpass all understanding,
All this stress in life,
Is sometimes too demanding,
Too much time plotting and planning,
You're the only one that can keep me standing,

Self preservations, ungodly relations
Making reservations,
For unrighteous indignation,
Democrats, republicans,
No consideration,
They lack the necessities,
To offer liberation,

Capitalist society,
Money often causes us to
Abuse our privileges,
Neglect our priorities
Manifested majestic,
We're not a minority
Though we're unaccepted,
We're still the majority.

No fruit in the labor of the corruptible seed,
Hunger and thirst, then die from greed,
Have no patience in those things they need,
Love your brothers, do good deeds,
You weren't chosen to follow
You were chosen to lead.

God so loved the world
He gave his only begotten son,
Why fight a war,
That's already been won
My life is full I'm having fun
Don't have to wait until the weekend comes,
When it's said and done,
And you've made your last run,
Heaven may have a ghetto,
But it has no guns.
Increase the peace
Through human relations,
Release the scars of degradation,
Peace among brothers of every nation,
From the least to the greatest,
Of GOD'S every creation
Prepare yourself,
"For the final destination".

Unreflecting Images

Unreflecting images,

That, reflect like glass,

Bound by images, that, reflect the past,

The opportunity, the chance,

The hope of sons,

Living in the fear of the evil one,

Their greatest agenda,

The agenda of flesh,

Mental anguish,

And spiritual distress,

Our environment refuses to humble,

Society's hostile,

In all spirit and truth and fullness of the gospel,

Only through, GOD are,

All things made possible

We become servants to ourselves trying to serve tradition

Serving a system,

That wants to make us

All victims, as the son of perdition,

We must be purged within,

Morally, thoroughly and spiritually cleansed,

Soldiers in a war

A battle for life,

Principalities, pride, envy, and strife,

An alliance designed,

To defeat the beast,

That, the weak would become strong and triumph in peace.

Unconstitutional Change

Unconstitutional change, the unwillingness of the wisdoms of man to become submissive, but
    only to his own ideas,
That, bring about boundaries which become their only concept to live.
The heart itself does not exist but beyond its own poverty.
Even in their own misbeliefs can be deceived of its own desires.
We ourselves are often times lost in our own confusion.
For each desire, becomes its own passion.
I suppose if things should ever change
The wars we ourselves fight within
Would be the greatest battles,
That leaves the greatest scars
Within, their own existence.
Each thought being processed
Of a knowledge as accessible as the life forms,
That was once but a thought itself
Projected to be light that becomes life that dwells
Within.
A world terrorized living in fear of its own confusion
But yet there's no illusion for life and death are only
Separated by a tenth of a second.
They keep falling in the battle fields of their own
Desires,
Un distinctive are the memories in the mist of war,
Reservoirs for pain,
A nation built in a bureaucracy of sin,
The discomforts of his own thoughts, that becomes a man.
A deeper knowledge
A greater understanding
For, we ourselves are but yet,
Victims, of our own ideas.
An apathy of pain that keeps us living in fear of our own ideas.
A nation constructed in the corruption of unconstitutional change

The walls that surround us hasn't yet been proven to withstand the winds of war,

Soldiers continuing to fall,

In a pawn of corruption,

An injustice that's possible may never be changed

Striving for a knowledge that's only but of an illusion of its own pain.

The starvation for powers

That are as illusive to man and greater than the knowledge wisdoms, and understanding of his own existence.

It's the insanity of the thought, that it, itself could be processed of its own understanding, as are the concepts of the mysteries that becomes vivid,

From the realities that are yet conformed of it's own ideas.

The metaphors of war has somehow become the only concept to live.

A constellation of thoughts that bring about, situations and circumstances that are but yet illusions themselves,

That bare not but only simulate the variances of life,

Only void of its own understanding,

And gives rebirth of the knowledge of its own existence,

That shall remain but a mystery

That will ultimately bring man to his uttermost destruction as the whisperings of the wind,

So shall they cease, as indicative as the matters before us,

A vindictive system of un resolve, and unrest.

Isolated in the inconsistency of our idle minds and souls

Where even our burdens are sometimes triumphant

In their own victories

It's the many in justifications of unconstitutional change.

The resurrection of life through death is said to be the formula for life

Life solidified through the separation of death.

Revelations becomes all but evident,

Of its call to judgment.

Even the most advanced technology is limited to boundaries

And void of its own existence as time itself cannot determine fate.

To glory in the success of our own being id but contemplation of death as eminent as the separation of the seas,

That, border the shores

Cold are the memories that sometimes become vivid

From the pain of war

A shadow of greatness as, are the skeletons of a closet for pain.

Infertile passion

The land's become desolate
The tree's without blooms,
Like running out of gas between
The earth and the moon,
Coming full circle, only to be
Confined to one room,
Infertile passions,
The un-bearing seed of an infertile womb.

Life or death

Don't fall to your desires but the fire within,
Don't let that, that condemns your soul,
Then condone your sins,
Condemnation abounds then locks you in,
What you've then found
Is a foundation for sin,
There's but one way out,
As but one way in
One judgment for all, once the sentencing begin,
Can you see the revelation?
The choices given to men
We're either sentenced to life,
Or death in the end.

Salvation of souls

I vision myself standing
On the shores that separates the
Seas and the oceans,
Staring out beyond the seas,
Exploring the depths,
It's like life sometimes spiraling out
Of control,
From the depths of my sins
To the depths of my soul,
Like the frost that leaves you
Bitten from exposure to cold,
There's no closure until I have
Reached my goal,
To preach and teach the
Salvations of souls

I surrender

This is the me, I never imagined I'd be,
God's will, reason, and purpose for me,
Though my trials and tribulations
Were often great,
There's but one who's perfect,
Who's without mistakes,
I've been called among many as a chosen few,
And for my father there isn't anything,
I wouldn't be willing to do
He did it for me he'll do it for you,
He couldn't lie to us if he wanted to,
He gave me the hope and inspiration
To make it through
Though I never imagined, he already know
Finally I'm able to understand
Only by grace and mercy was I able
To stand
I only possess the powers given
To man,
I surrender to his will, his vision,
His plan.

The birth of love

The birth of love,
The adoption of hate,
The option to believe and exercise
Your faith,
True love is unconditional
And well worth the wait,
First there was God
The defining of great,
Only God and, God himself
Who created heaven and earth
And life from death,
The reflection of light
Who became life himself,
He created the angels
To place by his side,
Hate assumed a face, an image, a pride, thrown from the heavens,
and assumed a disguise
An identity,
An enemy of love born from pride,
Given a heart and soul
It opened its eyes
It's knowledge and it's wisdom
Because unjustified,
The reason Jesus was sent
To be crucified,
That upon the third day
The truth would again rise,
The borders were established,
The lines were drawn,
Foundations were laid,
Seeds were sown,

Blood became flesh, flesh
Became bone,
Minds that could access,
That, detest their own,
Confess they're right,
When they know that they're wrong
Despite our own devastation
We must be strong,
Insight to revelations
The first to dawn,
Light separated from darkness
And assumed the throne,
Assumed command,
Consumed his own, there's no greater LOVE that's ever been known

Integrity

The integrity of a man,
Is based on his faith,
The sincerity of his heart,
When his world unravels, and begins
To fall apart,
Will he stand on the word
And still believe on God
Let not your spirit
Be troubled,
Your faith, wavered,
Or moved
Though the world can be,
Evil, wicked and rude,
Pervert not the right ways
Of the LORD,
Such ways are ways we should
Rightfully avoid
You've been established
In integrity
Confirmed through faith,
The integrity of a man
Is of mercy and grace.

Queen Mary

I'm the virgin Mary queen of all queens,
I gave birth to the vision,
That gives birth to your dreams,
Mother of Jesus
King of all kings
A child of God the father
Mother of Jesus the son
The virgin Mary
The world's #1 mom.

Live and let live

The values instilled
Can sometimes kill,
Should I as a man,
Impose my will,
Or give it to God and let him impose his,
It is what it is,
To live and learn,
Is to live and let live.

Whole

On my road to destruction,
There was a change of plans,
I decided to surrender,
To GODS never changing hand,
That he'd be just to forgive
And heal my land,
The LORD'S almighty
So think it not strange,
Tomorrow isn't promised,
Neither is the rain,
No man can change the LORD,
Or what the LORD'S ordained
He has mercy for man,
Because he has little for himself,
It's his will to increase
His faith,
And rebuild the little that's left,
That we would have abundance of life,
And dominion over death,
Come in from the darkness,
Out of the cold,
The Lord's doing a new thing,
Release the old,
He only seeks to redeem your soul,
Touch the hymn of his garment,
And be mad instantly whole.

Live by the sword

Though we've all been lost,
Minds unstable,
If you are willing,
He's more than able,
Not only have I received the promise,
I've obtained his favor,
Jesus Christ my lord,
And eternal savior,
The beginning of wisdom,
Is to fear the LORD,
Why seek ye him,
For a worldly reward,
Look ye unto heaven,
Where your treasures are stored,
His judgment isn't perverted,
Neither does his word return void,
He that lives by,
Must also die by the sword.

Jesus Christ is real

Faith will seal sins every leak,
Allow us to conquer every mountain,
By reaching its peak, reaching out
To God who neither slumbers nor sleeps,
And given us the charge to feed his sheep,
A charge we're all required to
Keep, walking in victory, never relenting defeat
In Christ we're given the zeal
A greater desire to do God's will
No affliction nor addiction
That faith won't heal,
Every knee must bow,
We all must yield,
The whole world must
Know Jesus Christ is real.

7 11

I rolled 7 and 11 but the devil held the dice,

Everything I won came with a price, and though I must admit,

They were more than nice, they melted before my eyes quicker than ice

But now I'm aware of his every device, I seek the kingdom of God, and eternal life

My faith is now in Christ the son, now faith is already done, faith makes ready the kingdom to come

TITLE:Everything I need/why should a man be grieved, if he has enough faith to trust and believe, JESUS CHRIST is every breath I breathe, everything I am, and everything I need!!!

TITLE: EXCEEDING GREAT REWARD/stand on GODS precious promises, and understand your rights, be strong in the LORD and the power of HIS might, the righteous of GOD is precious in HIS sight, for the love of CHRIST, we continue to fight, HE is the way the truth, and the life! One faith, one baptism, one LORD OF LORDS, HE'S given us HIS spirit, and HIS word as a sword, and promised HIS word won't return unto HIM void, for all those thing's we aren't able to afford, JESUS CHRIST is our exceeding great reward!!!